DATE DUE

5/12/04		
3/21/05		
MAY 29 2012		

Demco, Inc. 38-293

GODS AND PHARAOHS OF ANCIENT EGYPT

GODS AND PHARAOHS OF ANCIENT EGYPT

CHARTWELL
BOOKS, INC.

Published by Chartwell Books
A Division of Book Sales Inc.
114 Northfield Avenue
Edison, New Jersey 08837
USA

0-7858-0999-6

This book is produced by
Quantum Books Ltd
6 Blundell Street
London N7 9BH

Project Manager: Rebecca Kingsley
Project Editor: Judith Millidge
Designer: Wayne Humphries
Editor: Sarah Halliwell

The material in this publication previously appeared in
Egyptology, *Pyramids* & *Ancient Egyptians*

QUMEG&P
Set in Times
Reproduced in Singapore by United Graphic Ltd
Printed in Singapore by Star Standard Industries (Pte) Ltd

CONTENTS

CHRONOLOGY

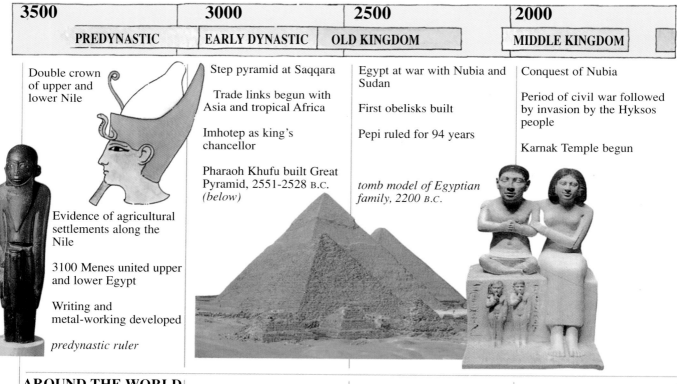

3500	3000	2500	2000
PREDYNASTIC	EARLY DYNASTIC	OLD KINGDOM	MIDDLE KINGDOM

Double crown of upper and lower Nile

Evidence of agricultural settlements along the Nile

3100 Menes united upper and lower Egypt

Writing and metal-working developed

predynastic ruler

Step pyramid at Saqqara

Trade links begun with Asia and tropical Africa

Imhotep as king's chancellor

Pharaoh Khufu built Great Pyramid, 2551-2528 B.C. *(below)*

Egypt at war with Nubia and Sudan

First obelisks built

Pepi ruled for 94 years

tomb model of Egyptian family, 2200 B.C.

Conquest of Nubia

Period of civil war followed by invasion by the Hyksos people

Karnak Temple begun

AROUND THE WORLD

Sumerians developed their form of writing

Growth of great cities in Uruk

Start of the Minoan civilization on Crete

Stonehenge in Britain

Indus Valley civilization flourished

Palace of Knossos built in Crete by Minoans

Growth of the Hittite Empire in Asia

1500	1000	500	A.D.	B.C.	500
NEW KINGDOM		**LATE PERIOD**	**GRECO-ROMAN PERIOD**		

Sea peoples (probably Greeks) invaded but were driven out by Ramses II

Kingdom divided: Libyan kings in the north, priests in the south

663 B.C., Egypt conquered by the Assyrians

Temple at Abu Simbel built *(left)*

525 B.C., Egypt conquered by Persians

Nectanebo, the last Egyptian pharaoh

Alexander the Great from Macedonia conquered Egypt

Ptolemy, the first Greek ruler of Egypt

Cleopatra, the last Greek ruler of Egypt, 48-30 B.C. *(below)*

Pharaoh Akhenaten *(above)* built a new capital city and tried to start a new religion. After 20 years, the city was abandoned and the religion failed.

Karnak and Luxor temples completed

Powerful pharaohs expanded empire with conquests over Nubia, Syria, and Palestine

Roman Emperor Augustus died, A.D. 14 *(above)*

Egypt under Roman rule until A.D. 395

Egyptians become Christians known as Copts

Mycenean empire ruled in Greece

Shang dynasty established in China

Celtic people arrived in Britain

Jews established kingdom of Israel and Judah

Beginning of Olympic Games

Classical Greek civilization at its height

Alexander the Great marches into India

Roman Empire included most of Europe and the Middle East

Start of the Byzantine Empire

INTRODUCTION

The Ancient Egyptian civilization lasted for many centuries, from around 3000 to 300 B.C. During that time, the Egyptians created massive buildings and elegant works of art. They invented systems of writing, measuring, and counting. They developed a strong, centralized government, served by scribes and officials. Egyptian designs and technological achievements were admired – and sometimes copied – in many countries of the ancient world. And their mysterious religious beliefs still fascinate scholars today.

In Ancient Egypt, as in many other civilizations, religion, politics, local tradition and everyday customs were mingled together. It is hard to discover in great detail what people really believed. Yet even though the Ancient Egyptian people lived so long ago, we can still find out about their lifestyles, customs and beliefs – their culture. Our information comes from different kinds of evidence – buildings, statues, tombs, towering pyramids, inscriptions, and many smaller objects – that have survived from ancient times.

The earliest Egyptians were nomads, wandering in search of food and water. But by around 2900 B.C., at the time of the first recorded Egyptian ruling family, they had been settled in villages along the banks of the Nile for hundreds, perhaps thousands, of years. The kingdom of Ancient Egypt grew up along the banks of the River Nile in North Africa. It was well-positioned for contact with both Mediterranean and Middle Eastern early civilizations. The River Nile provided a long strip of fertile land, perfect for growing crops. Including the Delta, it covered about 34,000 square kilometers. The Ancient Egyptians settled on its banks around 3000 B.C. and formed one of the most sophisticated early civilizations in history.

THE BEGINNINGS

From simple beginnings, the Egyptian state grew very strong. Egyptian kings, known as pharaohs, ruled a large empire. They fought and conquered far-away peoples, in present-day Syria, Libya, and Iraq. They traded with merchants from other ancient civilizations, such as the Lebanese and Greek, who lived around the Mediterranean Sea.

PRESERVED EVIDENCE

Thanks to Egypt's warm, dry, desert climate, many monuments have survived remarkably well. These tombs and temples were decorated with carvings, paintings, and statues. Some show everyday activities, others show religious scenes. They all tell us something about the way people lived – how they fought and farmed, went hunting, said their prayers, or simply enjoyed themselves. They also help us to discover what the Egyptians looked like, what they ate, and what clothes they wore.

Most Egyptian buildings, and many works of art, are decorated with inscriptions – lines of picture-writing called hieroglyphics carved into their hard-stone surfaces. Because stone is so tough, and lasts so long, these inscriptions can still be read, even after many

Facing page: Egyptian pharaohs were regarded as all-powerful by their subjects. In this tomb painting, a pharaoh is surrounded by paintings of various gods, who will protect him in the afterlife.

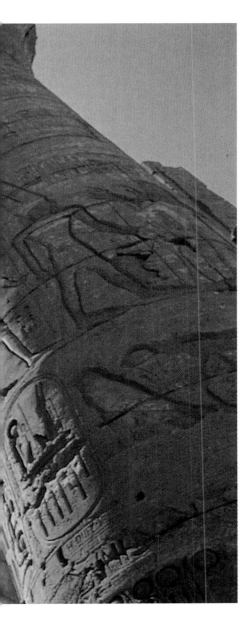

centuries have passed. Often they are a record of a great achievement, like building a temple or winning a war. The Egyptians hoped that these messages in stone would last forever. We can also learn about the Egyptians from travelers, such as the Greek writer Herodotus, who visited the country around 500 B.C.

GODS AND KINGS

The gods were a central part of Ancient Egyptian life. Evidence, such as a few prayers and early texts written on papyrus, tells us that the Egyptians worshiped many gods. These gods represented different qualities or aspects of life, and many took the form of animals, from bulls and cats to crocodiles.

Evidence also suggests that people at all levels of Egyptian society, from priests to peasants, were prepared to spend time and money on their religious beliefs. Pharaohs paid for elaborate tombs and temples; peasants gave food offerings, or purchased lucky charms.

HEAD OF THE PYRAMID

Egyptian society was arranged rather like a pyramid. The pharaoh was at the top. Then came high priests and nobles. Lower down were priests, officials, and army commanders. The fourth layer included skilled craftsmen. At the bottom came laborers and peasants.

To the Egyptians, their pharaoh was much more than just a king. He was the living image of a god come down to Earth. As such, he was respected, feared, and, occasionally, worshiped. The pharaoh was the only person who could speak directly to the gods in their temples. He gave them gifts of food and wine and, in return, asked them to send blessings to the people he ruled.

The most spectacular legacy of the pharaohs

Left: The temple was the home of the gods and needed to be of superhuman proportions. The columns of the Great Temple of Karnak are 79 feet (31.6 meters) high and 12 feet (4.8 meters) in diameter in places.

are the great temples they built. These were intended not for worship, but as homes for the gods. Many of these great temples, usually built on a monumental scale, still stand, and testify to the great respect Egyptians afforded their gods.

THE PYRAMIDS

The temples are not the only great monuments that testify to the skill and dedication of the Ancient Egyptians. From the golden desert sands, Egypt's pyramids soar into the air, proclaiming the power and majesty of the god-kings – the pharaohs – who built them. The pyramids served as magnificent royal tombs: within their stone walls, secret passages led to a chamber in which the casket of the pharaoh was placed.

Since the Ancient Egyptians believed in life after death, they buried the pharaohs together with a variety of objects for use in the next world, ranging from elaborate jewelry to wooden boats. It was the presence of treasures such as these that attracted robbers who, despite ingenious devices to deter them, almost always succeeded in entering and ransacking the tombs.

THE EARLIEST PYRAMID

Some of Egypt's great pyramids are more than 4500 years old. The first pyramid ever built was the step pyramid at Saqqara. And the greatest are the three that rise up from the desert near the Egyptian capital of Cairo. Of these, the largest is the Great Pyramid of King Khufu. The volume of this amazing structure is so vast that five huge cathedrals could be enclosed within its walls.

No one knows why the pyramid's triangular shape was chosen in the first place. It is possible that ancient peoples regarded it as

Left: Aerial view of the Middle Pyramid of King Khafra. At the apex is the remains of the original fine-stone casing.

holy because it pointed toward the heavens. The pyramids may even have been built to resemble mountains where the ancient gods lived. If this is the case, it is not surprising that temples were built on the tops of pyramids. This would have made the worshipers feel that they were closer to their gods. The Egyptians appear to have seen pyramids as staircases on which their dead kings could climb up to heaven.

THE MOST FAMOUS KING

The majesty of the pyramids and the Sphinx continue to leave visitors breathless almost four-and-a-half thousand years after they were built. The most famous and impressive tomb is that of the boy-king, Tutankhamun. The elaborate funeral mask of Tutankhamun, delicately crafted in gold and lapis lazuli, stunned the world when it was discovered in 1922. The combination of extraordinary riches, everyday objects, and statues of gods found inside the tomb is revealing about the beliefs of the Ancient Egyptians and their attitudes towards death, kingship, and the gods.

Left: The step pyramid of King Djoser at Saqqara is the earliest surviving pyramid. It was built around 2650 B.C.

Following page: King Khafra, builder of the Second Pyramid at Giza, reflects in his proud face the supreme power of the pharaoh. The hawk spreading its wings protectively around the pharaoh's head represents Horus, the god associated with kingship. (c. 2540 B.C.) (Cairo Museum.)

EGYPTIAN GODS AND GODDESSES

Bronze statuette of the cat goddess Bastet. (British Museum.)

Why did the Egyptians have so many gods? The gods of Ancient Egypt may appear to be strange, even frightening – but to the Egyptians themselves they were an essential and comforting part of their daily life, each one serving a particular need.

Above:Bronze figure of the sacred Apis bull. (British Museum.)

It is impossible to arrange Ancient Egyptian gods into neat categories, since their religious ideas were very complex. The sheer number of gods is staggering, since their religion developed over a very long period of time and they did not discard old beliefs when new ones became popular. From the earliest times, there were local tribal gods in various regions of the country, and some of these rose to great prominence during various periods of history. Often, for political reasons, many gods were also combined together as a means of consolidating their special powers.

BELIEF IN THE DIVINE

The belief in a divine power as an indeterminate and impersonal force universally present in all their gods was an essential part of Egyptian religious thought. Before gods had a particular form, or were given a name, the Egyptians would have worshiped the abstract concept of power.

The Ancient Egyptians' belief in the supernatural was closely interwoven with their daily lives, their personal relationships, their hopes and fears, and their attitude to the pharaoh's supreme authority. The day-to-day hazards of existence were believed to be the work of hostile powers, which could be suppressed by maintaining religious cults and preserving a divine order.

A VARIETY OF GODS

Some gods originated in ancient tribal traditions, such as the sacred bulls worshiped at

Above:: Glazed figure of the lioness goddess Sekhmet. (British Museum.)

Above: Wooden cosmetic spoon with handle decorated with the household god Bes, c.1300 B.C. (British Museum.)

Top right: This statue of the goddess Hathor, in the shape of a mother cow, was found in the tomb of Tutankhamun.

Bottom right: Statue wearing an emblem of the cat goddess Bastet. She gave life and fertility.

Apis, or the cats dedicated to the goddess Bastet, who gave life and fertility. Others, such as the sun god Ra, developed out of the Egyptians' reverence for nature. Some gods were honored throughout the land, others only locally. Some gods and goddesses had special functions. Pregnant women prayed to the goddess Taweret, for example, to keep them safe in childbirth. Farmers prayed to the gods of the Nile for floods to water their crops. Sekhmet was the goddess of war. She caused death in battle.

GODS OF THE HOME

Many other gods protected ordinary Egyptians, who worshiped them in their houses. Some of the gods had no temples dedicated to them, nor any given place in the official temple rituals. One of the most popular of these minor gods was Bes, who was depicted as a homely, ugly, dwarf god. Bes was regarded as a bringer of joy who warded off evil spirits and protected women in childbirth. The hippopotamus goddess Tauret also protected pregnant women, as did the cat goddess Bastet, and the cow goddess Hathor, who were also associated with dancing and music.

CHARMS

Representations of these household gods were used as decorative elements in the finer everyday items of the wealthy, such as beds, headrests, mirrors, and cosmetic pots. Images of the gods were thought to have supernatural powers, and the Egyptians wore many amulets to protect themselves. Many small faience charms were placed with their mummies to protect them on their hazardous journey to the next world, and their tombs contained models, statues, and paintings which had a similarly magical role.

ANIMAL GODS

Some gods looked human, while others had the heads of animals and birds. The Egyptians' apparent worship of animals should not be taken too literally, since animals could be used as convenient and familiar symbols to represent the attributes of various gods. Animal heads were placed on human bodies as a means of showing gods performing various rituals and relating them to human actions.

The worship of gods in the form of animals dates back to the earliest times in Egypt, and may have been motivated by humans' fear of

Right: Bronze statuette of the ram god Knum. (British Museum.)

Below: Kneeling bronze figure of a hawk-headed god. (British Museum.)

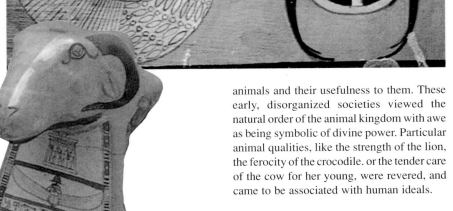

Above: The remains of a mummified baboon found at the temple of Thoth, Tuna el-Gabal.

Above right: This scarab (dung beetle) represented eternal life to the Ancient Egyptians.

Right: Rams were considered sacred by Ancient Egyptians. This mummified ram's head has been gilded and placed on a decorated board.

animals and their usefulness to them. These early, disorganized societies viewed the natural order of the animal kingdom with awe as being symbolic of divine power. Particular animal qualities, like the strength of the lion, the ferocity of the crocodile, or the tender care of the cow for her young, were revered, and came to be associated with human ideals.

ANIMAL MUMMIES

As time went on, many gods came to be depicted in human form. They still retained their identification with particular animals, however. By the Late period, almost every animal known to them was associated with one or more gods. The Egyptians worshiped animals kept at certain temples, like the Apis bulls at Memphis, or the cats at Bubastis. To

Above: Amenhopis III (who ruled from 1391 to 1351 B.C.) with his divine protector, the crocodile-headed god, Sobek. This statue comes from the Great Temple at Luxor.

Left: The jackal god, Anubis, who was the guardian of the dead. Painted relief from the tomb of Horemheb c. 1320 B.C.

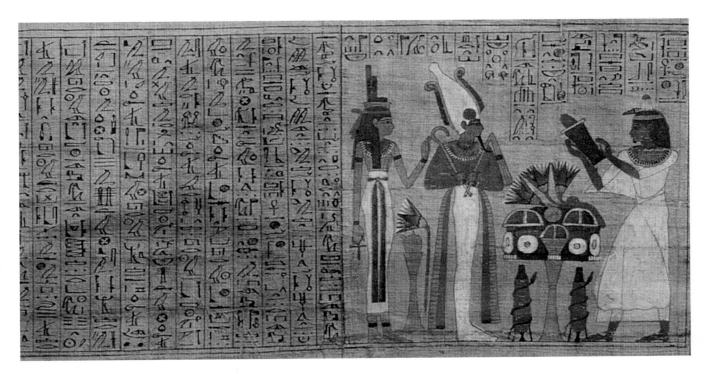

show their respect for the gods, they often turned these sacred animals, ranging in size from beetles to bulls, into mummies when they died, and buried them close to the temple. They thought that this would win them favors from the gods.

Some temples even bred animals specially for sacrifice and later mummification. Vast animal cemeteries were created at various centers of cult worship, and here people could show their devotion to a god by paying for the burial of its sacred animal. Thousands of dead hawks have been found at the temple dedicated to the hawk god Horus, in fields near his temple at Edfu.

The sky god Horus, for example, was depicted with the head of a hawk, while Anubis is shown with the head of a jackal. Anubis was believed to act as a guide to souls during their journey through the kingdom of the dead. Pharaoh Amenhopis III, who ruled from 1391 to 1351 B.C., was believed to have a divine protector called Sobek – the crocodile-headed god. Traditionally, Sobek had been worshiped in the marshy lake area known as the Faiyum – probably because many crocodiles lived there, and local people feared them. But gradually his cult spread throughout Egypt. Amenhopis gave generously to build temples, especially at Luxor, and many of these depict this formidable looking god.

Above: A king makes an offering to the gods. The writing describes how funeral ceremonies should be performed, and what each stage in the ceremony means. Egyptian scribes wrote many books, which have been preserved in the dry desert air. This page comes from the Book of the Dead. *Books like these provide valuable evidence about Egyptian hopes, fears and religious beliefs.*

Above: This statue of the sky god Horus, shown with the head of a hawk, comes from the temple at Edfu.

Right: Silver figure of the god Ra, with a falcon head and sun disk (British Museum.)

WORSHIPING THE GODS

Many gods were shown carrying symbols of their powers. In some centuries, certain gods were popular, while others were almost ignored. But one important religious belief hardly changed. This was the idea of *ma'at*: justice and order. The Egyptians believed that the gods ruled the world, and it was people's duty to live according to their will and to maintain *ma'at*, so far as was possible. For different groups in society, *ma'at* meant different things – soldiers had to fight bravely, peasants had to work hard, and

pharaohs had to rule well. Then the gods would be pleased.

SUPREME BEING

The opportunity for ordinary people to make offerings to the major gods only existed in later Egyptian history. Access to the temple interior was denied to everyone except the priesthood, and only after the Middle Kingdom (*c.* 2000 B.C.) were privileged people allowed to place votive statues in the outer courtyards. In general, the images of the gods were inaccessible to the Egyptian people, and any communication with them was exclusive to the pharaoh, or priests acting for him.

The king was believed to be a supreme being who maintained the unity and prosperity of Egypt. The destiny of the Egyptian people was linked to that of their pharaoh, and his welfare was also theirs. Worshiping their king was a means to encourage him to intercede with other gods on their behalf.

GODS OF TOWNS AND CITIES

Egyptian towns and cities served two main purposes: they were centers of government, and centers of trade. Many cities were also the home of a god, or, according to Egyptian religious belief, were regularly visited by one. The Egyptians believed in many local gods – "the spirits of the place" – who often took the form of typical local animals. The hawk-headed god Horus, for example, was particularly sacred to the inhabitants of Heliopolis. Other cities housed the shrines of major, national gods. At Thebes, for example, there was a magnificent group of tem-

Right: Khepri, the scarab-beetle god, from a painted casket, c. 1050 B.C. (British Museum.)

ples dedicated to the god Amun. And in the desert that lies beyond the opposite river bank, there were many royal tombs.

THE SUN GOD

In Egyptian mythology, the marsh vegetation, symbolized by papyrus and the lotus-shaped columns of a temple, represented the first solid matter, or mound, on which the god Ra appeared and created a pair of new deities, Shu and Tefnut, by masturbation or by spitting. They in turn produced the sky goddess Nut and the earth god Geb, whose children were the more familiar gods known as Osiris, Isis, Nephthys, and Set. Together, this group of nine gods ("ennead") was worshiped at Heliopolis. Other centers, meanwhile, had very similar groups of gods.

SUPREME GOD

Heliopolis was also the most important center of the cult of the sun god Ra, who was described in many texts as the creator of everything. The sun played a central part in religious beliefs throughout Egyptian history. The sun god Ra became important as early as the second dynasty (c. 2700 B.C.), and almost certainly had some connection with the building of the pyramids

By the fifth dynasty (c. 2400 B.C.), Ra had become the supreme state god who was very closely associated with the pharaoh. The king took the title "Son of Ra," and it was believed that after death he also joined his father Ra in heaven.

RENEWAL

Another belief was that the sun god was born every morning, aged and died, then traveled through the underworld during the night. This was seen as the model for all regeneration.

Ra was united with a minor Theban god called Amun to produce Amun-Ra, who became the supreme state god in the New Kingdom. From early times, Ra was also associated with the hawk god Horus, and the composite god Ra-Harakhty represented Horus of the horizon. The god of the morning sun was Khepri, who was identified with the beetle. The scarab beetle was thought to have created itself from its own matter as the sun seemed to create itself each morning.

Left: Bronze statuette of Imhotep, the architect of the earliest step pyramid at Saqqara. In later times ,Imhotep was worshiped as a god of wisdom. (C. 600 B.C.)

Above: Upper part of a large statue of Akhenaten (Cairo Museum). This is a stylized portrait of the most mysterious and individual of all the Ancient Egyptian pharaohs.

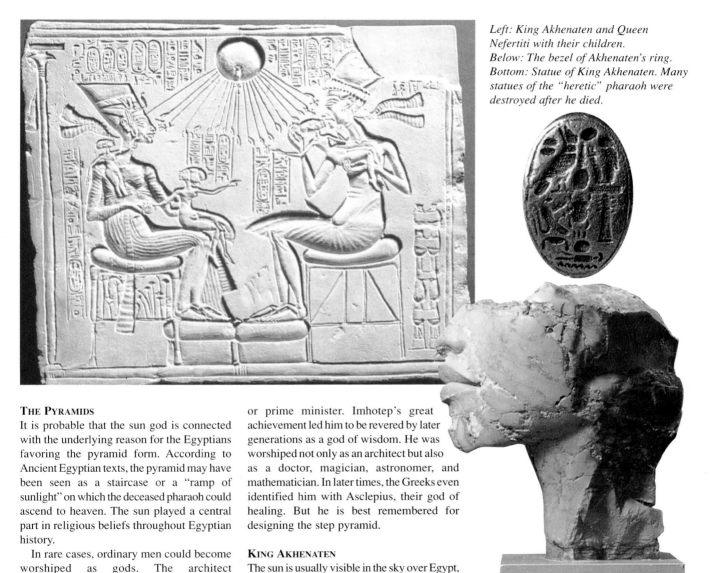

Left: King Akhenaten and Queen Nefertiti with their children.
Below: The bezel of Akhenaten's ring.
Bottom: Statue of King Akhenaten. Many statues of the "heretic" pharaoh were destroyed after he died.

THE PYRAMIDS

It is probable that the sun god is connected with the underlying reason for the Egyptians favoring the pyramid form. According to Ancient Egyptian texts, the pyramid may have been seen as a staircase or a "ramp of sunlight" on which the deceased pharaoh could ascend to heaven. The sun played a central part in religious beliefs throughout Egyptian history.

In rare cases, ordinary men could become worshiped as gods. The architect responsible for Pharaoh Djoser's step pyramid at Saqqara was Imhotep, the king's vizier, or prime minister. Imhotep's great achievement led him to be revered by later generations as a god of wisdom. He was worshiped not only as an architect but also as a doctor, magician, astronomer, and mathematician. In later times, the Greeks even identified him with Asclepius, their god of healing. But he is best remembered for designing the step pyramid.

KING AKHENATEN

The sun is usually visible in the sky over Egypt, and it is not surprising that it came to be worshiped. Toward the end of the eighteenth

dynasty (*c.* 1280 B.C.) there was a religious revolution in Egypt initiated by King Amenhotep IV, better known as Akhenaten. This new religion was based on the worship of the sun as the exclusive source of all life and creation, whose power was visible in the life-giving rays of the sun-disk called the Aten.

Akhenaten claimed to be the sole agent or high priest of the Aten on Earth, which gave him the right to disperse local priesthoods and close the temples of rival deities. The temples built for the worship of the Aten were architecturally different from the usual type, being open to the sky and without a sanctuary for a divine statue. It was Amenhotep III, Akhenaten's father, who first brought Aten worship to prominence, but Akhenaten ordered the complete exclusion of all the other gods. However, after Akhenaten's death, the old gods were reinstated at Thebes, and Akhenaten was regarded as a heretic.

KING OF THE DEAD

An essential part of Egyptian religion was the belief in life after death and the final judgement of the individual soul. The god Osiris was both king of the dead and judge of the underworld. In Egyptian mythology, Osiris was a good pharaoh who was murdered by his evil brother, Set. Osiris's death was eventually avenged by his son, Horus, and the king was eventually brought back to life, not as a human pharaoh, but as mummiform

Far left: The god Osiris – king of the dead, protected by falcons – from a painted casket, c. *1050 B.C. (British Museum.)*

Left: Sekhmet, the goddess of war, caused death in battle. Statue from the temple of Ptah at Luxor. Ptah, a creator god, was

king of the underworld.

Osiris had an important quality that made him more popular than the other gods. As a human king, he had experienced death and had triumphed over it, and therefore he could assure his followers an eternal life. It was believed that every king would become Osiris after he died, while his successor was the embodiment of Horus, his son.

ETERNAL LIFE

By the Middle Kingdom (*c.* 2000 B.C.), all worshipers of Osiris could themselves look forward to becoming an Osiris when they died, and would thereby enjoy eternal life. Abydos was one of the major centers of Osiris worship, and many Egyptians left inscriptions and offerings there to the god. Here they could witness the annual drama reenacting the death and resurrection of Osiris, most of which took place outdoors.

IMAGES OF THE GODS

The characteristic caskets in the shape of the mummified body with an idealized face mask mostly date from the New Kingdom or later. The stereotyped faces often had a false beard to symbolize their identification with the dead king Osiris. The coffins were painted with a representation of the sky goddess, Nut, who spread her wings protectively over the lid, since she was traditionally the mother of the deceased who was associated with her godly

often worshiped alongside Sekhmet, the destroyer.

Right: Gilded wooden figure of the god Ptah from Tutankhamun's tomb, c. *1350 B.C.*

Above: The River Nile, the life-blood of Egypt.

Right: Black granite statue of Hapy, god of the abundant River Nile. (British Museum.)

son, Osiris. Even the inside of the sarcophagus was richly decorated with images of the gods from the underworld, such as Osiris and Isis. This was done so that the dead person might have a fair judgement from these gods.

A TRIAD OF GODS

Osiris was also a god of vegetation, which may have been his original role. He embodied the yearly cycle of the renewal or rebirth of the land of Egypt after the Nile floods. His resurrection as king of the dead, and his renewal as a vegetation god were closely linked. The wife of Osiris, Isis, represented the devoted wife and loving mother, and was

GODS OF THE NILE

Certain gods were connected with Egypt's life-blood – the River Nile. The Nile was the natural habitat of the hippopotamus and the crocodile. Yet although they both became associated with gods, the hippopotamus was hunted with harpoons.

The beautiful temple at Kom Ombo was dedicated to Sobek, the crocodile god, and it is recorded that in 10 B.C. at Lake Moeris, Egyptian priests had a sacred crocodile which they tamed and fed with cakes and honeywine. Neither the hippopotamus nor the crocodile are to be found in the Egyptian river nowadays, as they have moved farther south, deep into the Sudan.

GIFT OF THE NILE

In Egyptian mythology, the Nile was like the River Styx of the Greeks, where the soul was ferried from the east to west bank. In their creation mythology, the first living matter could be likened to the fresh land after the flood. The Egyptians called their country "the gift of the Nile," and the annual flood was seen as the arrival of the Nile god, Hapy.

The gods worshiped by the Egyptians found their way into later cultures. The Romans, like the Greeks before them, absorbed many native religious beliefs after they conquered Egypt. They adopted Egyptian burial practices, developing both a sophisticated embalming technique and style of funerary portraiture. They also worshiped many Egyptian gods, although they often totally misunderstood their true nature.

The Romans imported many Egyptian statues and made many, often spurious, copies of them. Obelisks stood in the Temple of Isis and in the circuses in Rome. Since Rome became the most important city in the clas-

Above: Bronze figure of the god Horus as a Roman soldier. The Romans adapted many Egyptian gods into their own culture, without fully understanding their original religious function. (British Museum.)

Right: Mummy of a Roman boy. The Romans adopted the native Egyptian burial customs and added naturalistic portraits to them. (British Museum.)

a very popular goddess of magic who continued to be worshiped in Roman times. Osiris, Isis, and Horus represented a family unit and a triad of gods.

Similar groupings of three existed among many other Egyptian gods. The most notable other triads of gods were worshiped at Thebes – Amun, Mut, and Khons – and Memphis – Ptah, Sekhmet, and Nefertum. Osiris received general acceptance throughout Egypt, and was not only a state god but also a popular god to whom ordinary people could relate.

sical and Christian world, the Roman selection and interpretation of Egyptian forms strongly influenced the way in which the rest of Europe viewed Ancient Egypt. Consequently, the knowledge handed down to medieval and Renaissance Europe was largely governed by what interested classical and Byzantine scholars.

INFLUENCE ON CHRISTIANITY

It is often demonstrated that the Christian religion contains many practices and images which had their roots in pagan Egypt. This is quite understandable since, during the formative years of Christianity, the religious rituals inherited from the Romans were already steeped in Egyptian traditions. When the powerful Roman Empire officially adopted the new Christian religion, it embraced many existing concepts and images. In particular, the cult of Isis, strong in the early Roman Empire, could have provided a prototype image of the Virgin and Child through the many representations of Isis suckling Horus. It is recorded that an original ancient statue of Isis survived in a French church until the sixteenth century; in a different French church, meanwhile, the birth of Isis continues to be celebrated today.

CHRISTIAN IMAGES

The popular representation of Christ triumphant over harmful beasts bears a striking resemblance to the image of the Egyptian god Horus triumphant over the crocodile. Many similar parallels can be drawn between the portrayal of certain Christian saints and Egyptian gods, while holy attributes like the halo, crook, and the idea of winged humans as angels also have Egyptian precedents.

The central Christian emblem, the cross, is often represented on early Coptic monuments as the Egyptian ankh sign of life and is still clearly present on medieval tombstones in the Balkans. Many subconscious Egyptian elements would have been conveyed by the bishops from Egypt, who were highly influential at the early church councils in Rome.

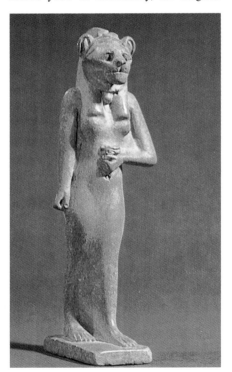

Far left: Glazed figure of the lioness goddess Sekhmet. (British Museum.)

Left: This gilded bronze figure of Isis and Horus provided the universal image of mother and child. (British Museum.)

EGYPTIAN PHARAOHS

Above: One of the most famous
objects to survive from Ancient Egypt – the
gold burial mask of King Tutankhamun.

T he word "pharaoh" comes from the Egyptian *Per-aa*, meaning "Great House," and originally referred to the royal palace rather than the king himself. It was used by the biblical writers and has become widely adopted since as a special word for the king of Egypt. The pharaoh had several official titles which related to his unique status as being both god and king. He was referred to as the son of the god Ra, and the name of Ra is usually mentioned within his two royal seals or cartouches, along with his personal name. He was also believed to be the incarnation of the god Horus, the son of Osiris, who, in Ancient Egyptian mythology was the first king of the world.

Above: Head, probably of Queen Hatshepsut, carved from fine green schist, wearing a tall white crown. (British Museum.)

Right: This pyramid, built by Pharaoh Khephren (2520-2494 B.C.), is considered the "true," or perfect, architectural design for pyramids. The Sphinx, half human and half lion, lies on guard.

The pharaoh is also constantly referred to as being the "Lord of the Two Lands." In early times, the people of Egypt were gathered in the north and south. The unification of these two geographical regions under one pharaoh's rule became a primary event in Ancient Egyptian history.

Although a new capital was established at Memphis, there continued to be a northern and southern center of government administration, and throughout Ancient Egyptian history there is evidence of a deep-seated awareness that the one nation had been formed out of the two lands. The Ancient Egyptians achieved a national unity through the pharaoh, which brought them all the benefits of a centralized nation, and enabled efficient irrigation, land reclamation, and pyramid building.

SON OF THE SUN

Royal pedigree was not an essential qualification for kingship in Ancient Egypt, and the divine nature of the pharaoh's office rendered any mortal connection secondary. The king's accession to the throne was justified by his claim to be son of the sun god, Ra, rather than the son of a preceding king. In taking up the very office of pharaoh, he had in effect an unquestionable right to the throne of Egypt. Ay and Horomheb, for example, had no royal pedigree, yet they each succeeded Pharaoh Tutankhamun, and could justify their kingship through this principle.

All Egyptians had legal rights, and could own or dispose of their possessions. There was no system of citizenship or slavery, as clearly defined in Greece and Rome. Egyptian society never produced a true middle class, and the social structure was a hierarchy of officials where everyone ultimately served the pharaoh, who was the embodiment of the state.

PHARAOHS AND THEIR PEOPLE

To the Egyptians, their pharaoh was more than just a king: he was the living image of a god come down to Earth. As such, he was respected, feared, and, occasionally, worshiped. The pharaoh was the only one who could speak directly to the gods in their temples. He gave them gifts of food and wine and, in return, asked them to send their blessings to the people he ruled.

As well as having religious duties, an Egyptian pharaoh was responsible for running the government. He had to maintain law and order, protect temples, and lead his armies to war. A pharaoh also had to be good at managing people. He needed to win the support of powerful nobles and chief priests to stop them plotting against him.

The pharaoh also had to make sure that his government officials used their power to benefit the country, not just to make money

for themselves. He received foreign ambassadors in his palace, and made peace treaties with kings and princes from distant lands. Often, this meant marrying a foreign princess to strengthen the alliance. Some pharaohs had a great many "official" wives.

Royal women in Egypt were respected as the wives and mothers of pharaohs – and therefore the wives and mothers of gods. Once, when a king of Babylon asked Pharaoh Amenhophis III for one of his daughters as a wife, Amenhophis haughtily refused. "The daughter of the king of Egypt is not given to anyone," he said.

A GREAT QUEEN

Among the most famous of the powerful Egyptian women was Queen Hatshepsut. The pharaohs of the New Kingdom, and in particular those of the eighteenth dynasty, have aroused the greatest popular interest, and Hatshepsut was one of the first notable pharaohs during this period. She ruled the country from 1473 to 1458 B.C. as the dominant partner and personality in a coregency with her nephew and stepson, the young Thutmose III.

Hatshepsut is frequently depicted on statues and reliefs with the male attributes of royalty, including the false beard. During her reign, Senenmut, the chief steward, assumed a position of great power as her favorite, and supervised the building of her magnificent temple at Deir-el-Bahari in Thebes.

PHARAOHS' CROWNS

Pharaohs, and sometimes gods, were portrayed wearing several different types of crown. Each crown had a special meaning. On ceremonial occasions, pharaohs also wore a false beard, made of tightly plaited hair, ornamented with

Above: Queen Hatshepsut's Temple, a complex of colonnaded shrines, rises in terraces to the cliffs at Deir-el-Bahri.

gold and jewels. The white crown was traditionally worn by kings of upper Egypt – the lands in the southern part of the country. The red crown was traditionally worn by kings of lower Egypt, the marshy northern lands around the Nile Delta. Ever since Pharaoh Menes, who came to power around 2920 B.C.,

the two kingdoms of upper and lower Egypt had been ruled by one pharaoh. To make this clear, many pharaohs chose to be portrayed wearing a double crown, that is, the red and white crowns together. A smaller, blue war crown was worn whenever the pharaoh led troops into battle.

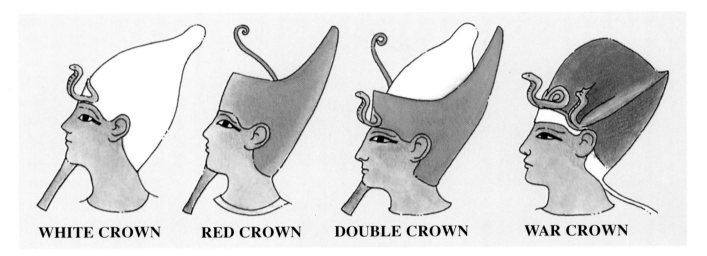

WHITE CROWN **RED CROWN** **DOUBLE CROWN** **WAR CROWN**

THE PALACES

The pharaohs' royal palaces were vast, sprawling buildings. So many people lived and worked there that they were more like little villages than family homes. There was a great reception hall, where the pharaoh received royal visitors, listened to his advisers, and granted – or refused – requests from petitioners groveling on their knees. There were also private rooms and luxurious bedrooms for the pharaoh and his family, offices for his ministers, guardrooms, and quarters for soldiers and servants.

Egyptian palaces were built of dried mud-bricks, which does not sound very glamorous. But life inside was elegant, comfortable, and luxurious. Royal palaces could be two or three stories tall. Hollow channels between the floors allowed cool breezes to circulate, a simple form of air-conditioning; it would have been very welcome in the noon-day heat.

By the time of the New Kingdom, many palaces had toilets, and even showers; water was sprinkled from large jars balanced overhead. After a shower, pharaohs and their families would retreat to the nearby "oiling room," where their skins would be massaged and softened by smooth, scented oils.

ENTERTAINMENT

Pharaohs and their courtiers were entertained at feasts in the palace by dancers and musicians. Favorite instruments included harps, drums, and cymbals. Egyptian dancers were well-trained and acrobatic. Tomb-paintings show dancers performing cart-wheels, somersaults, high-kicks, and even the splits. Other entertainments included wrestling and story-telling.

RULING EGYPT

The geography of Egypt makes it a difficult place to rule. It is a very long country, about 745 miles (1200 km) from north to south. Apart from a narrow, muddy strip of land along both sides of the river – and even this is sometimes

Above: Pharaohs were portrayed wearing several different types of crown. Each crown had a special meaning. A white crown was worn by kings of upper Egypt, while red signified kings of lower Egypt. When the two kingdoms were joined, many pharaohs wore a double crown. Pharaohs wore a blue war crown whenever they led their troops into battle.

Above left: Dancing girls often entertained the pharaohs and their courtiers.

Above right: Musicians also provided entertainment for the pharaohs. The harp was a favorite instrument of the Ancient Egyptians.

flooded – the land is desert. In ancient times, there were hardly any roads. The best way to travel was along the river, but this was very slow. It could take about three weeks to reach Nubia from the city of Memphis. How could the pharaohs keep control?

Successful pharaohs coped with this problem of government in two different ways. They relied on trustworthy local governors – chosen from among noble families, or top officials – to rule the provinces for them, and they recruited an enormous number of scribes. The scribes, along with certain other officials, sent and received royal messages, and kept detailed records of everything that concerned government, law, and taxes. Many of these records have survived. They can tell us a lot about how the Egyptian government worked.

EGYPTIAN SCRIBES

It took a long, slow training to become a scribe. Trainees started young – before they were 12 years old – and were made to work very hard while learning. Sometimes they were beaten – the Egyptians had a saying: "A boy's book is on his back."

Egyptian scribes wrote on paper called papyrus that was made from reeds, and used ink made of soot. Sometimes they also decorated their writings with red ink. The Egyptians were among the earliest people in the world to invent writing, in around 3000 B.C. They wrote using picture-symbols – hieroglyphics.

HIEROGLYPHICS

Some hieroglyphs stood for the sounds that make up words, others stood for ideas, or for actual objects. For example, the hieroglph for the sounds we make when we say "r" was an open mouth. The hieroglyph for the idea of drunkenness was a pot of beer.

Scribes had to combine several hieroglyphs to "spell" each word in the documents they were writing. Hieroglyphs could be written across or down the page, and words were "spelled" without vowels. Scribes also kept records of tribute payments. Tribute – paid in food, treasures, or by sending men to work – was collected by the pharaoh's officials from ordinary people.

PHARAOHS AND WAR

Pharaohs also had to lead their people in war. The Egyptian government was well-prepared for fighting. The pharaohs maintained a standing army, lodged in barracks in important cities. These troops were tough, well-fed, and fit. Warfare was brutal. Pharaohs, wearing a special crown, led their armies into battle surrounded by hand-picked troops. Not all pharaohs went to war, however, although many were portrayed fighting.

The early Egyptians fought with bows and arrows, spears for throwing, heavy wooden clubs, and axs. Chariots, curved swords, and body armor were introduced later on. Usually a chariot was manned by two soldiers, a driver and an archer, armed with arrows and spears. Egyptian warships, which were driven by oars as well as sails, were faster

Left: Painted limestone statue of a scribe in the traditional, cross-legged pose, with his papyrus scroll unfolded in his lap. (Cairo Museum.)

PHARAOHS AND EMPIRES

After the collapse of royal power at the end of the Old Kingdom, the successive pharaohs of the Middle Kingdom had to contend with the increased strength and arrogance of the provincial governors. The country was divided into a number of administrative districts called "nomes" under these governors, who had transformed their offices into hereditary principalities. Perhaps to limit their power, the Middle Kingdom kings developed a centralized hierarchy, and the royal residence was moved from Thebes to Lisht, which was a more convenient center for ruling the country.

For hundreds of years, the Egyptians raided parts of Nubia, which was rich in gold and other natural resources. In a tomb painting, Nubians bring gifts of precious stones and leopard skins to Pharaoh Thutmose IV.

These reforms enabled King Senusret III to raise a sizeable army for his Nubian campaigns, when the frontier was moved farther south and was protected by a network of fortresses. This was the first main period of expansion. Egyptian troops occupied Nubia, a land rich in treasures – gold, ebony, ivory, leopard skins, and black African conscripts. In another campaign, during the New Kingdom, Senusret increased the hold Egypt already had over Palestine and Syria.

THE HYKSOS

During the short reigns of some 70 weaker kings of the thirteenth dynasty (*c.* 1786-1633 B.C.), bureaucracy increased, and the lack of a strong government enabled a group of Asiatics called the Hyksos to invade and control Egypt for around a century. The Hyksos introduced some important technical innovations – bronze-working, the horse and

Above: This wall-painting shows a pharaoh wielding a battle-ax, clutching captives. Not all pharaohs went to war, however, although many were portrayed fighting.

Above right: A kneeling bronze figure of a pharaoh offering two ointment jars, c. 1420 B.C.

and easier to steer than enemy craft.

After the time of the Hyksos invasion, Egyptian craftsmen copied designs for deadly, high-powered bows from their Asian neighbors. Most soldiers carried shields, did not wear helmets, and fought barefoot. They aimed to scatter the enemy by a sudden, fierce attack. Both sides in a battle fought to kill. But if any of Egypt's enemies were captured alive, the men were forced to fight in the Egyptian Army, or were sent to work as slaves.

chariot, and other weapons of war, such as more powerful bows.

THE NEW KINGDOM

The first pharaohs of the New Kingdom drove out the Hyksos rulers and unified the state with a much improved economy. They went on to extend Egyptian territories into Western Asia as far as the Euphrates. The Egyptian "Empire," which included the city states of Syria and Palestine, paid tribute but remained self-governing, while Nubia was administered directly by the Egyptians through an appointed viceroy. Trade and Nubian gold produced much of the country's wealth and power in international relations, and the surviving royal burial treasures display unprecedented wealth and aesthetic beauty.

Thutmose III continued the policy of foreign conquest with campaigns in Palestine, Syria, and Nubia. Many impressive buildings and important private tombs were created during his reign, which are a sign of the economic benefits of his imperialistic policy. Late in his reign he turned against the memory of Hatshepsut, and ordered many of her statues and reliefs to be defaced or usurped by his own name and image. His actions were perhaps due to the Egyptian concept of kingship as being exclusively male, rather than due to personal hatred of his aunt.

THE SUN KING

Under Amenhotep III, Egypt continued to be acknowledged as a superior power by her Asiatic neighbors. In Syria, the kingdom of Mitanni sent princesses as a gift of tribute to the pharaoh, and peace brought great prosperity to Egypt. There was an unprecedented output of architecture and sculpture on a grand scale during his reign, much of it

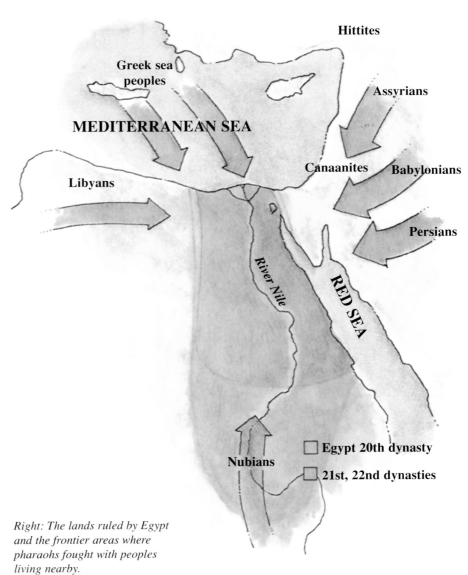

Right: The lands ruled by Egypt and the frontier areas where pharaohs fought with peoples living nearby.

Above: Standing statue of a pharaoh from the Middle Kingdom – his thoughtful and concerned expression is characteristic of the style of portrayal during this period. (British Museum.)

Right: King Mentuhotep was the first pharaoh of the Middle Kingdom. He reigned for 50 years and restored order to the land of Egypt.

of superb quality. Amenhotep III was succeeded by Amenhotep IV, who is more commonly known by the name Akhenaten from his association with the sun cult of Aten.

THE HERETIC PHARAOH

Akhenaten came to be regarded as the "heretic pharaoh," since he broke with a long established religious tradition of worshiping many gods, choosing instead to adopt a single faith. He believed that the Aten was the universal creator of all life, and its visible symbol were the rays of the sun. He became totally preoccupied with spreading his new faith, and this meant that he neglected affairs of the state and military involvement.

In order to disassociate and distance himself from the powerful existing priesthood at Thebes, Akhenaten built a completely new city some 900 miles (300 km) down the river at El Amarna. Here he built a palace to house his court, and Amarna became the new capital and religious center for the worship of the Aten.

Akhenaten appears to have been very interested in the arts, and beside composing various hymns to the god Aten, he encouraged the development of an entirely new, more naturalistic art style. Unfortunately, very little has survived, since after his death he was proclaimed a heretic and his city was systematically destroyed, and his monuments ruined and defaced.

Several pieces of royal portrait sculpture were discovered, however, among them the bust of Nefertiti which has come to be regarded as one of the most famous Ancient Egyptian works of art. Various diplomatic correspondence has also been discovered at Amarna, which reveals the disorder within the Egyptian Empire. There are desperate pleas

for assistance from royal kingdoms under attack from the Hittites, which the pharaoh appears to have ignored.

THE MOST FAMOUS PHARAOH

After Akhenaten's death, the heir to the throne was Tutankhaten, whose exact relationship to him has not been fully established. When Queen Nefertiti died shortly after Akhenaten, the priests of Amun seized the opportunity to persuade the boy-king to renounce his faith and reinstate the worship of the original gods at Thebes. To acknowledge this, the ending of his name was changed, and he then became known as Tutankhamun. The old ways were gradually restored, and the city of Amarna was abandoned for Thebes.

The usual preparations were made for the pharaoh's tomb in the Valley of the Kings at Thebes, but Tutankhamun died young, before

Above: Gilded wooden figure of a king, probably Amenhotep III, wearing a plaited wig, c. 1400 B.C. (British Museum.)

Right: Painted plaster bust of Queen Nefertiti. Carved in the naturalistic style used during the reign of her husband, King Akhenaten, this is one of the most beautiful and famous images in Egyptian art, c.1365 B.C. (W. Berlin Museum.)

*Above: The gold mask of Tutankhamun
(c. 1350 B.C.).*

*Previous pages: Ramses II in his chariot
attacks the Hittite fortress of Dapur, in
Syria. Reconstruction of a painted relief
from the Ramesseum, Thebes, c. 1270 B.C.*

its completion. It was therefore necessary to
bury him in a makeshift tomb whose
modesty and less obvious location caused it
to be overlooked by the tomb-robbers.
Although it was broken into hurriedly, and
with little loss early on, it remained intact for
more than 3000 years. The immense public-
ity the discovery of his tomb received in 1922,
and the sheer wealth and beauty of the arti-
facts, has made this historically insignificant
boy-king the most famous pharaoh of all.

AFTER TUTANKHAMUN
Tutankhamun left no heir to succeed him, and
an important and powerful official called Ay
briefly became pharaoh. He was followed by
a successful general called Horemheb, under
whom all trace of the Akhenaten heresy was
erased from Egyptian history. The city of
Amarna was destroyed, and the royal
cartouches of Akhenaten and Tutankhamun
were erased from the temple records.

SETI
The first notable pharaoh of the nineteenth
dynasty (c.1320-1200 B.C.) was Seti, who con-
solidated Egyptian power in Palestine, and successfully resisted the Hittites, with whom he
signed a peace treaty. He instigated a vast pro-
gram of building, and his temple at Abydos
contains numerous superb bas-reliefs which
are regarded by many as the finest examples
of Egyptian art. This style of relief sculpture
was also used to decorate his tomb, which is
the largest and most beautiful in the Valley
of the Kings. Toward the end of his reign, Seti
I shared his throne with his son Ramses II,
who became the greatest pharaoh of all.

THE GREAT RAMSES
Ramses began his reign with a military

campaign in Syria, where he fought the Hittites
at the notorious battle of Qadesh. There are
numerous depictions of the battle on temple
reliefs which show it to be a great Egyptian
victory, but it is generally believed to have
been an indecisive battle. Shortly after it, a
truce was made, which was confirmed by mar-
riages between Ramses and Hittite princesses,
and this continued for over 50 years.

ART AS PROPAGANDA
Ramses may have used art as a means of pro-
paganda, and his victories over foreigners are
depicted on numerous temple reliefs, while
he had more colossal statues than any other
pharaoh. He also usurped many existing
statues by inscribing his own cartouche on
them.

This same cartouche is carved on every
significant group of ruins in Egypt, and probably half the surviving temples have additions
by him. Many of these great building projects
date from his early years, and it appears that
there was considerable economic decline
toward the end of his long, 66-year reign. The
pharaoh was nearly 100 years old when he
died, and was the father of about 90 children
by numerous wives.

Of the nine succeeding kings who have the
same name, Ramses III is probably the most
notable. He inherited a stable internal situa-
tion and built an impressive and beautifully
decorated temple complex at Medinet Habu.
He defeated an attempted Libyan invasion and
renewed attacks by the so-called "sea peoples" of the Mediterranean. As the pharaoh
proudly reported, his ships defended the coast
"like a strong wall." Ramses III also boasted
that he had seen his enemies "overthrown in
their blood, and made into heaps."

POWERFUL ARMIES

Throughout the New Kingdom, the authority of the pharaoh was affected by two new forces in Egypt's internal politics: the priesthood and the army. The king, as the traditional protector of Egypt, was assisted in police and military matters by an army.

The armies of the New Kingdom were far greater and more organized than in previous times with their chariots, infantry, and marines. The army was organized into four divisions of about 5000 men each, which gradually became composed of more mercenaries, such as Nubians, Asiatics, sea peoples, and Libyans. Prisoners-of-war could win freedom by taking up service in the pharaoh's army, and at the Battle of Qadesh, Ramses II's army included contingents of Mediterranean soldiers who had been captured in previous wars.

Although military strategy was always credited to the pharaoh, he would have consulted a war council of officers and high state officials before embarking on a campaign. This kind of general staff would have had great experience in controlling large numbers of men, which was probably why they were considered qualified to take over kingship at various times during the eighteenth dynasty when the pharaoh had no direct heirs. Ay, Horemheb, Ramses I, and Seti I had all had military training, and when the country was drifting into anarchy in later periods, army officers stepped in to restore order.

FOREIGN DOMINATION

By the twenty-first dynasty (*c.* 1085-945 B.C.), the country had become divided between two ruling houses. A group of kings established a new capital at Tanis in the Delta, while much of upper Egypt was controlled by generals who made themselves the high priests of Thebes. A significant pharaoh during this period was Psusennes I. The beautiful treasures from his tomb, which were discovered by Pierre Montet at Tanis in 1941, have been compared in their quality and richness to those of Tutankhamun. Political weaknesses led to foreign domination, first by Libyan kings of the twenty-second dynasty, then by the Ethiopians of Nubia in the twenty-fifth dynasty.

The pharaohs of the next dynasty established a new capital at Sais and restored order in Egypt. During this period of economic stability and great prosperity (*c.* 664-525 B.C.), there was a rebirth of art, architecture, and literature influenced by the earlier periods of Egyptian history. Some of the art of this

Below: Scribes kept the pharaoh's records.

period reached a highly stylized perfection, and there was a tremendous output of fine - quality small-scale sculpture.

CLEOPATRA

The rule of the Saite pharaohs was brought to a close by the Persian invasion and domination during the twenty-seventh dynasty. In 332 B.C., Alexander the Great conquered Egypt and his principal general, Ptolemy, set up a dynasty of pharaohs based at Alexandria. This new city on the Mediterranean coast became a major trading center, and its famous lighthouse and library made it a wonder of the ancient world. The Greek domination of Egypt continued until Queen Cleopatra was defeated at the Battle of Actium in 31 B.C. and Egypt became a province of the Roman Empire.

A FAMOUS FIGURE

Through literary tradition, Cleopatra has captured popular imagination as a beautiful and scheming queen. She was a member of the Ptolemaic dynasty – ruling family – of Egyptian kings and queens. They had originally come from Greece, but had been settled in Egypt for around 250 years. She was the seventh Egyptian queen to bear the name of Cleopatra, and although her ancestry was Greek, she spoke the Egyptian language and shared some of their religious beliefs.

Cleopatra's affairs both with Julius Caesar and Mark Anthony, and her final suicide, were associated with her struggle to retain control of Egypt. She killed herself when the Romans conquered Egypt because she preferred a noble death to foreign rule.

A QUEEN'S ROLE

Cleopatra ranks with Hatshepsut and Nefertiti as one of the best-known queens of Egypt.

Some of the principal queens had a powerful position in Egyptian society, second only to the pharaoh. The king was allowed to marry several wives, but the most important was called the "Great Wife," and her children were usually the only heirs to the throne. Queen Hatshepsut was the daughter of King Thutmose I and his "Great Wife."

The "Mother of the King" continued her title as wife and queen when her son became pharaoh, but she in turn became subordinate to the new king's principal consort, the "Great Wife." The eldest son of the pharaoh by this principal queen often became his heir. Intermarriage among the Egyptian royal families was not as widespread as has been claimed, and was really a political union to contain power within the family and reinforce succession.

FOREIGN PHARAOHS

Certain foreign conquerors, notably the Macedonian Greeks, realized the benefits of depicting themselves as traditional native pharaohs in statues and on monuments throughout Egypt. They also had their names translated and placed in the customary royal cartouche, and thereby claimed their divine ancestry alongside preceding kings. They were able to gain the maximum revenue from the country that they, or their predecessors, had conquered by assuming this supreme position of both god and king.

Above: Head of Cleopatra, c. 50 B.C. (British Museum.)

TEMPLES AND TOMBS

Above: The Great Temple of Karnak. Its columns are 79 feet (31.6 meters) high ,and 12 feet (4.8 meters) in diameter in places. The temple was the home of the gods, and therefore needed to be of superhuman proportions.

"**B**ehold, the heart of his majesty was satisfied with making a very great monument..." This inscription on the temple of Pharaoh Amenhophis III at Luxor explains why the Egyptians created these magnificent buildings. The "very great monument" demonstrated the pharaoh's power. It showed religious devotion and revealed good taste. Most importantly, as a monument to the pharaoh and his gods, a temple would last for ever.

Above: The temple at Karnak became the biggest and richest in Egypt. The temple is guarded by great statues of Ramses II.

TEMPLES FOR THE GODS

The massive Egyptian temples were not intended for community worship like European cathedrals. Most Egyptian temples were arranged like palaces, because a holy statue of the god "lived" or visited there. Their main function was as home of the gods. The temple, with its gateway, courts and halls, was built around one small room, the sanctuary, housing the statue used by the god as its resting place.

STATUES OF THE GODS

These statues did leave the temples for special religious festivals, when they could be approached by ordinary people, but their images were still hidden in a shrine carried on a sacred boat. Sometimes the statue was taken from one temple and moved to another, or was carried in procession through the streets or in boats along the Nile. Daily rituals in the temple included the washing and clothing of this divine statue by the senior priests, and the offering of incense and food before it.

Pharaohs were religious leaders as well as being heads of government and leaders in war. They took part in such important ceremonies, especially on festival days. Together with priests and nobles, the pharaoh would escort the procession of the statue of the god through the temple courtyards to the sanctuary. The Egyptians did not worship the statue itself. Rather, it reminded them of the presence of the god, whose invisible spirit might come to them at any time.

RELIGIOUS RITUAL

The significance of this ritual was symbolically to maintain the divine order of daily life, and it did not represent blatant idol worship. In the carved reliefs in the temple, the king himself is always shown performing these rituals. In practice, however, priests would usually have taken over this role.

Such reliefs were usually carved with great skill, and often occur even at the top of walls and columns, where they could not be seen. They were not intended to beautify the building or inspire the worshipers, but had an entirely magical function. In addition, the columns, ceilings, and floors were all thought to have magical powers that could be invoked by rituals.

A MODEL CREATION

The temple was not only seen as a symbolic representation of the world, but was also built as a model of its creation. The wavy tiers of mud-brick walls surrounding the sacred precinct probably represented the primeval waters, while, inside the enclosure, the rows of papyrus and lotus-shaped columns symbolized the earliest marsh vegetation.

ABU SIMBEL

One of the greatest Egyptian temples was built by Pharaoh Ramses II (1290-1224 B.C.) at

Above: The Egyptians used hieroglyphics to carve inscriptions in stone columns.

Right: We can make good guesses at what palaces and temples looked like. They were built with magnificent "hypostyle halls" – rooms where the roofs were supported by carved and decorated columns. Often they were painted to look like reeds.

Above: The dramatic temple entrance at Abu Simbel.

world to help them save their important Nubian monuments from the flooding due to the construction of the colossal Aswan High Dam, built between 1960 and 1970. An international consortium of contractors and archeologists was set up to move the huge temple of Abu Simbel, and some other monuments, to high ground. The vast rock temples were cut into 30-ton blocks and then reassembled at an identical site above the level of the lake. Similarly, the beautiful temples of Philae were painstakingly transferred stone by stone to a nearby island, safe from the flood-waters of the Nile.

TEMPLES FOR THE PHARAOHS

Not all temples were palaces for the gods. Some were built over royal tombs, to worship the memory of dead pharaohs, and to glorify their achievements in this life. Queen Hatshepsut arranged for a beautiful mortuary temple to commemorate her time in power. Built around 1450 B.C., it contains almost 200 statues portraying episodes during her reign. It is carved partly out of the solid rock face, and was originally surrounded by gardens, trees, and statues. It is decorated with carvings showing scenes from Queen Hatshepsut's eventful life.

TOMBS FOR THE KINGS

The mummy's eternal dwelling-place was the tomb. The type of tomb varied according to the period, the area, and the owner's social status. It is important to remember that the vast majority of poor Ancient Egyptians would have had a simple burial in the desert with few possessions. The tombs of the privileged who could afford a more elaborate burial were either built of stone and brick, or cut out of the solid rock. They all generally

Abu Simbel in Nubia. The temple is guarded by four huge statues of Ramses himself. Twice a year, rays from the sun shone inside the temple and lit up the carved statues of gods.

Thousands of years after the temple was built, an Italian explorer called Giovanni Belzoni discovered an entrance to the Second Pyramid and the Tomb of Seti I, in the Valley of the Kings. He also traveled south to the great temple of Abu Simbel, which he was the first to enter since ancient times.

THE ASWAN HIGH DAM

In the 1960s, the Egyptians appealed to the

consist of two main parts: the burial chamber and the funerary chapel.

The Old Kingdom tombs had a false door which served as a magical entrance through which the spirit of the deceased could pass from the burial chamber on the western side of the tomb into the chapel on the east. Here the spirit could partake of the offerings of food and drink provided by relatives or priests.

ROYAL CASKETS

Few royal caskets have survived, but the evidence is that they were of gilded wood, inlaid with stones and glass paste. Surviving intact examples are the three-nested caskets of Tutankhamun. They were enclosed in a rectangular stone sarcophagus decorated inside and out with funeral gods in painted relief.

One of the finest stone sarcophagi is that of King Seti I, which is of white calcite inlaid with rows of funerary figures in blue paste. The kings of the twenty-first and -second dynasties from Tanis (c. 950 B.C.) were buried in mummiform caskets of silver and gilded wood, two of them with silver hawks' heads.

MUMMIES

Inside the great tombs of the Egyptians lay mummies. The Egyptians mummified dead people in the hope of providing them with everlasting life. While their bodies survived, their spirits would also. But in preserving their dead people as mummies, the Ancient Egyptians have also helped to keep alive the memory of their magnificent civilization for many thousands of years.

Mummies are perhaps the most famous and intriguing type of evidence to have survived from Egyptian times. It is an extraordinary feeling to be able to look at the face of somebody who lived over 4000 years ago.

Above: Ramses II's statues in the forecourt of the Luxor temple.

Left: Some caskets were carved from stone, like this fine basalt example made for a vizier, c.500 B.C. (British Museum.)

A wall-painting from the tomb of Sennedjem, who lived around 1300 B.C. It shows him, with his wife Iyneferti, busily occupied after death. Above them, the hawk-headed god Horus holds the ankh, the symbol of everlasting life.

The outer casings of a mummy, and the casket or sarcophagus in which it was buried, can tell us about the Egyptians' religious beliefs, and, sometimes, about the long, complicated funeral ceremonies they arranged. We can discover how old the mummified person was when they died, some of the illnesses they had suffered from, and, probably, how wealthy they had been. We may even be able to find out what individual Egyptians looked like, or more accurately, how they wished to be remembered for ever more.

Left: The so-called "Colossi of Memnon": gigantic, seated statues of the Pharaoh Amenhotep III, originally part of his mortuary temple at Thebes, c. 1400 B.C. (British Museum.)

MAKING MUMMIES

Making the mummies was a skilled and unpleasant process. Bodies rotted quickly in the hot sun. Many ordinary people could not afford a beautifully decorated mummy or casket; their bodies were preserved as quickly and cheaply as possible. In contrast, the families of important people lavished a great deal of money and time in preparing the best possible mummy for their dead relative.

Mummies often had more than one casket: for example, Tutankhamun had four. They were made from wood, which was then heavily decorated on the outside with both paint and gold leaf. Mummies were made by specialist workers, who became very skilled at their gruesome job. First they removed the soft tissues – the heart, lungs, stomach, intestines, and brain – from the body. These were preserved separately, in canopic jars. Each was mixed with scented gum and sealed in a separate jar; hawk-headed jars held intestines. Then they packed the body with natron, a chemical which dried and preserved it.

TO LAST forEVER

Bodies were kept in natron for up to 60 days – the longer, the better. Then they smeared the dried body with sweet-smelling oils and gums, and sprinkled it with herbs. All these helped to preserve it. Noble bodies also had face masks, often made from gold and precious stones. These were representations of what the dead person looked like. Finally, the mummy's limbs were arranged in a dignified way, and it was tightly wrapped in bandages and cloth. Now it could be placed in its decorated casket and was ready for burial. Hopefully, it would last forever.

THE TOMB OF TUTANKHAMUN

The discovery of Tutankhamun's tomb was one of the most exciting events in twentieth-century archeology. Explorers knew that many rulers of Ancient Egypt had been buried in the Valley of the Kings, but they also knew that most of these graves had been robbed long ago. Tutankhamun's tomb had itself been disturbed at some time in the past, but the robbers had failed to discover the secret burial chamber where the mummified body of the young pharaoh lay hidden. For 35 centuries, knowledge of Tutankhamun's grave was lost.

During the nineteenth and early twentieth centuries, many explorers traveled to Egypt, hoping to discover more about its past. Howard Carter, the British archeologist who discovered Tutankhamun's tomb in 1922, spent many years of his life studying the remains of Ancient Egypt. Even with his expert knowledge, he was still amazed at the richness and beauty of the objects he found in Tutankhamun's tomb chambers.

A THRILLING DISCOVERY

An extract from a newspaper report of the finding, published in 1922, records the thrill of the discovery: "Cautiously, the explorers edged their way along the narrow passage. They had no idea what lay ahead. They had already passed one sealed door. Now they came to another. Using a heavy iron spike, Carter cut a small hole at eye-level, so he could see (by flickering candlelight) into the next chamber. Eagerly, he peered into the gloomy darkness. Then he turned to Lord Carnarvon, his voice shaking with excitement: 'I see wonderful things …' he said." Later, Carter remembered that day (November 25, 1922) as "the most wonderful I have ever

Above: Egyptians believed that the souls of the dead were carried to the next world on funeral boats. This boat was found in the pyramid at Giza.

Right: The mask that covered the face of Tutankhamun was made of solid gold and inlaid with precious stones. It is believed closely to resemble the actual face of the young king.

Above: One side of a painted chest found in Tutankhamun's tomb. The sphinxes represent the king as he treads his enemies underfoot.

scientists have suggested that disease-causing fungi may lurk in the ancient tombs, although we do not know for certain that they caused Carnarvon's death.

A GLORIOUS RESTING-PLACE

Tutankhamun's burial chamber reveals the immense wealth of the ruling royal family which prepared his tomb. His grave is probably the most famous and best-preserved of all Egyptian royal burials. Yet despite its splendor and lavishness, this tomb may not have been unique. The types of object found there are typical of royal and noble status in this world, but also were designed to help him in the world of the dead.

A plan of the tomb shows four separate chambers. Each chamber had a ritual purpose: the east room was for rebirth; the south for eternal royalty; the west for departure toward the funeral destinies; and the north for reconstitution of the body. There are two lifesize guardian figures inside the tomb. They are made of wood, varnished black, with the features and clothing gilded.

PROTECTED BY THE GODS

The face of Tutankhamun's mummy was covered with a magnificent funeral mask made of pure gold, decorated with many precious stones and with colored glass. The goddess Hathor, in the shape of a mother cow, watched over the body of the dead king. She wears the sun disk between her horns. The pharaoh's coffin was decorated with pictures of the many gods and goddesses who, the Egyptian people hoped, would protect Tutankhamun's soul in the next world of the dead.

The precious objects put into a tomb alongside a dead person were chosen with great care. They included food and drink, models

lived through."

Lord Carnarvon, the wealthy patron who financed Carter's explorations, died suddenly and unexpectedly not long after Tutankhamun's tomb was discovered. People said that he had died as a result of the "Mummy's Curse" – the dead pharaoh's revenge on anyone who dared to disturb his tomb. In fact, Carnarvon died from infection following a mosquito bite. But recently,

Right: This gilded box in the shape of a double seal is made of gold-plated wood inlaid with glass paste. It was found in the tomb of Tutankhamun.

Far right: The face of one of the two life-size guardians of Tutankhamun's tomb. He is made of wood, varnished black, with his features and clothing gilded.

Right: An elegant model boat from Tutankhamun's tomb.

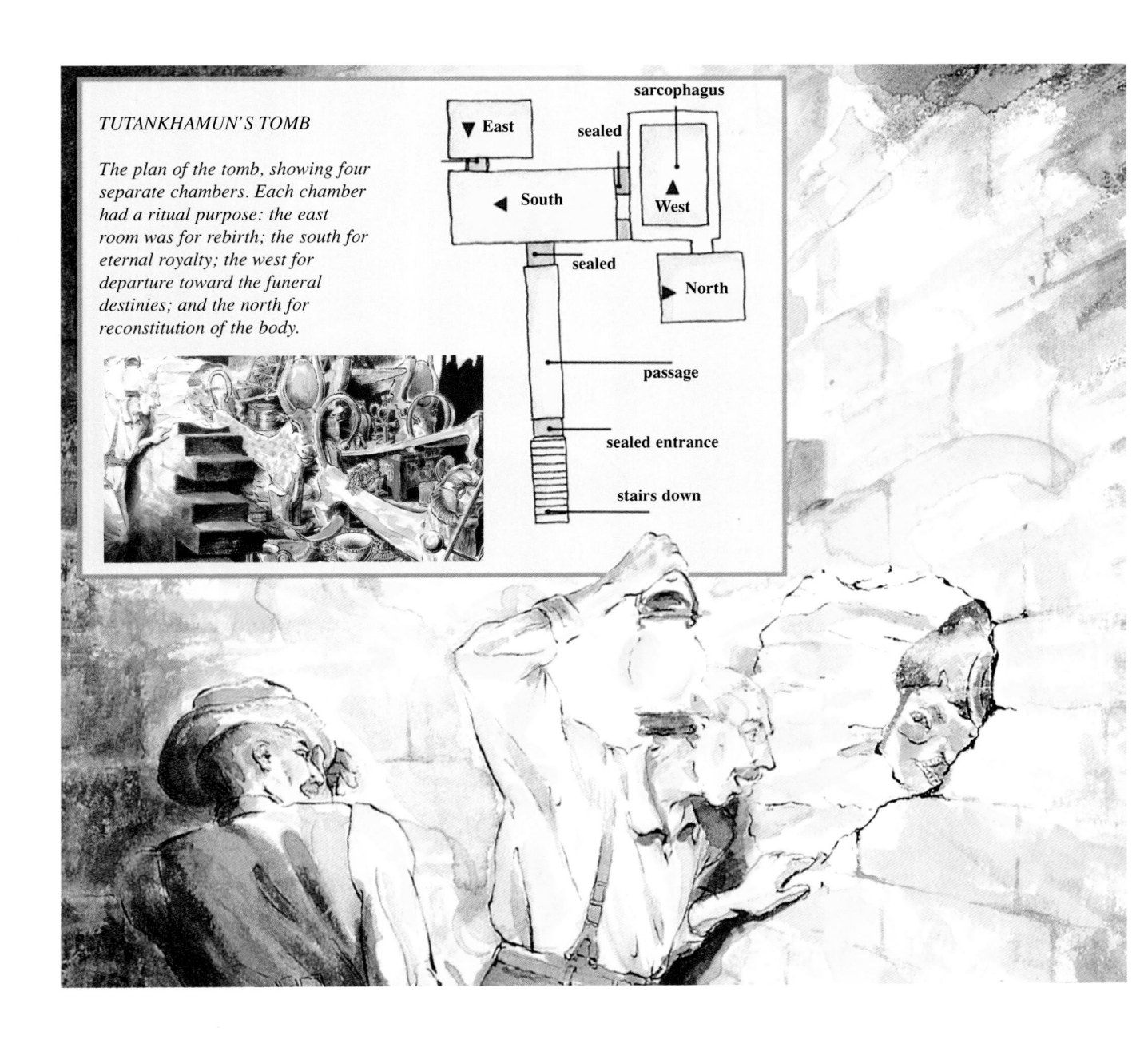

TUTANKHAMUN'S TOMB

The plan of the tomb, showing four separate chambers. Each chamber had a ritual purpose: the east room was for rebirth; the south for eternal royalty; the west for departure toward the funeral destinies; and the north for reconstitution of the body.

sarcophagus

▼ East

sealed

▲ West

◄ South

▶ North

sealed

passage

sealed entrance

stairs down

of servants and guards, and even means of travel: Egyptians believed that the souls of the dead were carried to the next world on funeral boats.

All these different objects were placed inside the tomb because the purpose of an Egyptian burial was to help the dead person live again "for millions and millions of years." Life on Earth was uncertain and sometimes sad; true happiness was to be found after death. The Egyptians believed that by carefully preserving a dead body, you would also preserve its spirit, and give it everlasting life.

A HOUSE OF ETERNITY

A tomb was therefore a "house of eternity." Often, important people designed their own tombs while they were still alive. Tutankhamun did not do this, probably because he died so young. For him, royal officials provided everything his spirit might need for its everlasting life, from food and drink to musical instruments and fans. But this new life was not lived in the tomb itself. That was simply where the body was kept. Tutankhamun's spirit, like everyone else's, had to travel to another world – the peaceful kingdom of the dead. And so the officials included all that his spirit needed for this last, dangerous journey – boats, guardian statues, clothes, and weapons.

Right: The Tomb of Queen Nefertiti – *watercolor copy by Nina Davies (1881-1965).*

THE END OF THE EMPIRE

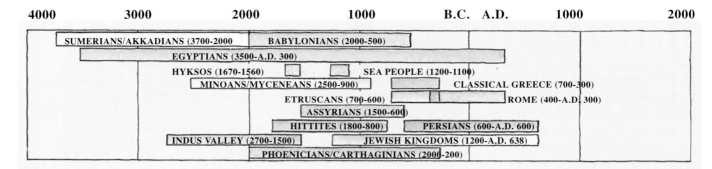

4000	3000	2000	1000	B.C.	A.D.	1000	2000

SUMERIANS/AKKADIANS (3700-2000   BABYLONIANS (2000-500)

EGYPTIANS (3500-A.D. 300)

HYKSOS (1670-1560)   SEA PEOPLE (1200-1100)

MINOANS/MYCENEANS (2500-900)   CLASSICAL GREECE (700-300)

ETRUSCANS (700-600)   ROME (400-A.D. 300)

ASSYRIANS (1500-600)

HITTITES (1800-800)   PERSIANS (600-A.D. 600)

INDUS VALLEY (2700-1500)   JEWISH KINGDOMS (1200-A.D. 638)

PHOENICIANS/CARTHAGINIANS (2000-200)

After about 1100 B.C., Egyptian power began to decline. This was for several reasons; discontent at home, enemies abroad, and the impact of new technology. For many years, from about 1100-950 B.C., Egypt was divided in two. Libyan merchants ruled the north, while temple priests, based in Thebes, controlled the south. Then Libyan soldiers, paid to guard the desert frontiers, rebelled. A Libyan high priest, Sheshonk, became pharaoh, and ruled successfully for many years. But more troubles followed.

ATTACK OF THE NUBIANS

Around 730 B.C., the Nubians invaded, and conquered land as far north as Thebes. In 663 B.C., Assyrian armies attacked. They were armed with iron weapons, and swiftly won control. A cunning Egyptian prince, Psammeticus, negotiated a peace treaty, and, shortly afterward, took over. He invited foreign merchants to come and settle in Egypt, in the hope that they would help him

rebuild Egypt's wealth and power. In the short term he succeeded, but Egypt's new prosperity made the land an even more attractive target for would-be conquerors.

SUCCESSIVE INVASIONS

Invaders came again in 525 B.C. Persian troops attacked, and established a new ruling family, which governed for almost 200 years. It was overthrown by the armies of Alexander the Great, a very successful war leader from Macedon in northern Greece, in 332 B.C. When Alexander died, it was arranged for a Greek ruling dynasty, called the Ptolemies, to succeed him.

Under the rule of Augustus (30 B.C.-A.D. 14), Egypt became prosperous. Trade increased, as the people of Rome were eager to buy corn. The Roman rulers introduced new laws and heavy taxes, which the people hated. Through contact with Rome, Egyptian ideas, especially in mathematics and medicine, together with religious beliefs, spread beyond

Above: The Egyptians were not the only great civilization in the Middle East. In this chart, you can see the names of Egypt's neighbors, and the times when they were powerful.

Egypt and throughout the Roman empire.

The end of independent Egyptian civilization finally came in 30 B.C., when Cleopatra, the last Ptolemaic ruler of Egypt, committed suicide rather than be taken prisoner by Roman troops loyal to the emperor Augustus. Not long afterward, Egypt was declared to be a province – colony – of Rome.

In 624 A.D., the remains of Roman control were swept away, and Egypt became part of a mighty new Muslim empire, based in Damascus and later Baghdad. Under Muslim rule, Egypt became a rich and flourishing state. The Egyptians did not fully regain their independence until 1952.

Right: Coin showing the Roman emperor Caesar Augustus (30 B.C.-A.D. 14), the conqueror of Egypt.

Below: Nubian soldiers, from an Egyptian tomb model. They are well-armed with bows and arrows.

Above: Egypt today. Under Muslim rule, Egypt became a rich and flourishing state during the Middle Ages. This is the great city of Cairo. In the distance you can see the citadel (fortress) ,topped by a graceful mosque.

Right: A Greek "portrait mummy" made for a Greek settler in Egypt. People often paid for portraits to be painted showing them looking young and well-dressed. After death, these were used to decorate their mummies.